QUIET DIVERSITY

A Guide to Cultivating Introvert-Friendly Workplaces

SARA YAHIA

Original Version: English
Publication: February 2024
Last Edit: January 2026

DEDICATION

To the quiet strength and wisdom of introverts:

Cultivating introvert-friendly workplaces is not just important; it's essential. In a world where silence speaks volumes and authenticity holds unparalleled power, we must ensure that every voice gets the space to be heard and valued.

"Silence is the new loud,
and authenticity is our battle cry."

Sara Yahia

TABLE OF CONTENTS

CULTIVATE QUIET BRILLIANCE

Dear Readers,

In today's evolving work environment, the call for inclusivity is louder than ever, urging organizations to celebrate diverse talents and working styles. At the heart of this movement lies the need to create workplaces that are friendly to introverts.

Quiet Diversity champions the often-overlooked strengths of introverts: depth of thought, intentional communication, and the ability to see what others miss. These are not softer versions of extroverted traits, but distinct forms of intelligence that thrive beyond noise and spectacle.

When organizations recognize these capabilities, the impact is unmistakable. Decisions improve, burnout declines, and innovation becomes sustainable rather than performative.

As you explore these chapters, you will uncover strategies designed to disrupt conventional thinking and position so-called limitations as advantages.

As an introverted HR expert, I wrote this guide to help companies foster equity. This book celebrates the dynamic interplay of diversity, inviting organizations to embrace the richness that stems from truly inclusive practices.

Thank you for joining me on this journey. I hope *Quiet Diversity* inspires you to recognize and appreciate what often sits outside the spotlight, thereby creating a more engaging and fulfilling professional landscape.

"The greatest loss in modern organizations is not a lack of talent, but the insight that goes unheard."

Quietly Yours,
Sara Yahia

THE QUIET POWER WITHIN

CHAPTER 1

UNDERSTANDING INTROVERSION

Human Resources leaders hold the power to shape supportive workplaces. Introverted individuals possess valuable qualities, including deep thinking, creativity, and attention to detail.

Research suggests that introverts can make meaningful contributions to innovation and productivity.

For example, the University of California found that introverted employees excel in roles requiring solitary work and in-depth problem-solving.

However, introverts may struggle in environments that prioritize extroverted traits. Approximately 30-50% of the workforce identifies as introverted. Overlooking their needs can lead to lower job satisfaction and output.

By recognizing and appreciating these unique attributes, HR leaders can tailor recruitment and employee development strategies.

Ultimately, managerial teams will foster a culture where all employees thrive. This understanding enhances employee well-being and retention, maximizing the potential of the entire workforce.

A Gallup study indicated that organizations with inclusive practices have a 21% increase in profitability and a 33% increase in employee engagement. Both introverted and extroverted employees are crucial for sustainable success.

KEY CHARACTERISTICS OF INTROVERTS

Introverted individuals exhibit characteristics distinct from those of extroverts. Introversion exists on a spectrum, with expressions varying from one person to another. Here are some common observed qualities:

SELECTIVE STANCE: They regulate their energy by deciding when and with whom they invest attention, where mental bandwidth is easily fragmented. Instead of pursuing widespread visibility, they optimize for relational precision, connecting through shared values rather than fleeting momentum.

INDEPENDENT SOULS: Introverts process information internally before broadcasting it. Ideas are pressure-tested, refined, and stress-scanned before entering discussion. Given uninterrupted time, they produce original, high-fidelity views, driven by depth of analysis, not speed of response.

WRITTEN SKILLS: They may feel more comfortable expressing themselves in writing than verbally, where precision and nuance can be fully shaped.

THOUGHTFUL DECISION-MAKING: They tend to be cautious, carefully weighing options and outcomes, prioritizing long-term impact over immediate reaction.

PASSIONATE INTERESTS: They often pursue specific interests or hobbies with sustained commitment and passion, developing depth rather than breadth of expertise.

BUILDING TRUST SLOWLY: They prioritize authenticity, cultivating meaningful relationships through consistency rather than speed.

These tendencies are influenced by upbringing, lived experiences, and personal differences.

MYTHS AND STEREOTYPES

Introversion has given rise to various myths and stereotypes. Dispelling these misconceptions is crucial for a more accurate understanding of introverted individuals. Here are some common myths and their realities:

MYTH: INTROVERTS ARE SHY

REALITY: Introversion is not the same as shyness. While some introverts may be shy, it is primarily a preference for less stimulation and more solitude. Introverts can be outgoing and confident, but may find extended social interactions draining.

MYTH: INTROVERTS ARE ANTISOCIAL

REALITY: Introverts are not antisocial. They enjoy socializing in moderation and prefer meaningful conversations over large, boisterous gatherings. Introverts invest in people selectively.

MYTH: INTROVERTS LACK LEADERSHIP SKILLS

REALITY: Introverts can be inspirational leaders. They excel in active listening and fostering a positive work environment, driven by emotional intelligence.

MYTH: INTROVERTS CANNOT SPEAK IN PUBLIC

REALITY: Introverts can be skilled public speakers. Although they may avoid the limelight, many can deliver powerful presentations by connecting with their audience.

MYTH: INTROVERTS DO NOT LIKE TO HAVE FUN

REALITY: Introverts enjoy fun on their own terms: balancing social engagement with downtime.

Introverts are keen observers of context, which shapes their style of levity. Their cleverness emerges through dry wit, subtle irony, or playful remarks. What may appear as seriousness is often discernment: an intentional choice.

MYTH: INTROVERTS LACK CONFIDENCE

REALITY: Introverts can be confident; however, their confidence may manifest differently than that of extroverts. They often shine with meticulous preparation.

MYTH: INTROVERTS ARE UNFRIENDLY

REALITY: Despite their reserved demeanor, introverts can be warm, friendly, and approachable once comfortable. They value authentic relationships.

MYTH: INTROVERTS DO NOT LIKE TEAMWORK

REALITY: Far from fading into the background, introverts can subtly steer team dynamics, ensuring every voice is heard and reaches its full potential. They detect blind spots, ask the questions no one else does, and turn group chaos into focused action.

Debunking these misconceptions cultivates a more understanding workplace. The strengths of both introverted and extroverted individuals contribute to a collaborative and supportive culture in which everyone can thrive.

Introverts don't hide in the shadows…

They quietly run the show.

THE SPECTRUM

The introvert-extrovert spectrum is a framework for understanding personality traits related to social behavior and energy preferences.

Rather than being strictly dichotomous, it acknowledges that individuals exhibit varying degrees of introverted and extroverted characteristics.

INTROVERSION: Characterized by an internal orientation toward cognition and energy management. Prolonged external stimulation taxes focus, while independent work environments enable sustained concentration and deliberate contribution.

EXTROVERSION: Defined by a need for external stimulation and social interactions. Extroverts gain energy from being around others and feel invigorated by group activities. Outgoing by nature, they flourish in collaborative environments.

AMBIVERSION: Describes individuals who display introverted and extroverted traits. Ambiverts adapt their behavior to fit different situations, exhibiting both ends of the spectrum depending on the context.

In addition to these broad categories, there are distinct types of introverts, reflecting specific nuances in their preferences.

SOCIAL INTROVERTS: They engage comfortably but with boundaries. They participate fully, then disengage to reset. Their strength lies in social calibration: knowing when presence adds value and when restraint preserves clarity.

THINKING INTROVERTS: They operate in a cognitively rich inner environment. They have an abstract reasoning that generates solutions that emerge fully formed rather than incrementally discussed.

ANXIOUS INTROVERTS: Often uneasy in group settings, they fear judgment and scrutiny. They are cautious and excel in roles that require attention to detail and empathy. Their sensitivity steers a caring work culture.

RESTRAINED INTROVERTS: Methodical and deliberate, they assess before acting. Stability and reliability define their influence, bringing order to fast-moving or unpredictable settings.

Visibility is secondary to enduring results.

The introvert-extrovert spectrum reveals diverse personalities. While broad categories provide a general understanding, examining the specific factors influencing each type of introvert offers deeper insights into their unique behaviors.

FACTORS INFLUENCING BEHAVIOR

Positioning on the introvert-extrovert spectrum is not static; it can shift depending on the context. This variability suggests that our responses adapt to different situations.

LIFE STAGES AND SELF-AWARENESS: Personal experiences significantly influence how personality is expressed. Career demands may encourage extroverted tendencies, while aging may foster more introverted behaviors.

Case Study: Jake Thompson, who initially leaned toward extroversion due to his leadership role, shifted toward introverted behaviors as he approached retirement. He began focusing on self-examination and mentoring, illustrating how career demands and personal growth shape personality.

EXPECTATIONS AND NORMS: Cultural expectations can impact how introversion and extroversion are displayed. These lenses shape not only how individuals behave but also how their strengths are recognized, rewarded, and integrated within social and professional spheres.

Collectivist Cultures: Societies with communal norms often value introverted traits such as thoughtful reflection. In many East Asian cultures, introverts align with ideals of wisdom and respect.

Individualist Cultures: In cultures that emphasize individualism, such as many Western societies, sociability and assertiveness are more celebrated. In the U.S., extroverted actions are highly valued, which can marginalize introverts and pressure them to adjust.

Case Study: At TechGen Solutions, a multinational firm, the leadership team adapted communication strategies to accommodate cultural preferences, improving team cohesion and productivity. This highlights the advantages of recognizing cultural diversity in the workplace.

The interplay of individual, situational, and cultural factors affects personal development. Embracing diverse cultural backgrounds fosters better communication, benefiting employees and organizations.

Being an introvert is not a limitation; It's a unique asset.

By integrating the rich spectrum of introverted traits, we can unlock human potential and create environments where everyone can thrive.

Let's celebrate introverts and work toward a future that values every voice and thrives through inclusivity. Onward to a more innovative tomorrow!

CHAPTER 1 - QUIZ

Welcome to the quiz in Chapter 1: *Understanding Introversion*. This quiz assesses your comprehension of the key concepts and insights presented in this chapter.

Reinforce your understanding of how introverts impact workplace dynamics, their unique characteristics, and the importance of an inclusive environment. Good luck!

1. As an HR leader, you notice several introverted employees are disengaged in meetings and avoid collaboration. Which approach best applies the understanding of introverts to improve engagement?

a) Schedule mandatory large-group activities to force participation.

b) Provide options for small-group discussions and let input come naturally.

c) Assign them to high-profile client-facing roles immediately.

d) Encourage extroverted colleagues to mentor them socially.

2. What qualities are often associated with introverts?

a) Deep thinking, creativity, and attention to detail.

b) Sociability, assertiveness, and spontaneity.

c) Outgoing nature, enthusiasm, and extroversion.

d) Risk-taking, impulsiveness, and high energy.

3. You are assigning project roles and need to match tasks to personality traits. Which assignment best leverages an introverted employee's strengths?

a) Lead a high-traffic, client-facing sales campaign.

b) Analyze complex data and develop a detailed report independently.

c) Host a weekly all-hands meeting.

d) Facilitate a fast-paced networking event.

4. What percentage of the workforce identifies as introverted?

a) 10-20%

b) 30-50%

c) 50-70%

d) 70-90%

5. What myth about introverts is dispelled by recognizing their ability to enjoy social interactions in moderation?

a) Introverts are shy.

b) Introverts dislike people.

c) Introverts are antisocial.

d) Introverts lack leadership skills.

6. Which of the following characteristics is often observed in introverts?

a) Preference for large group gatherings.

b) Thriving in noisy environments.

c) Reflective thinking.

d) Spontaneous decision-making.

7. What is the reality regarding introverts and leadership skills?

a) Introverts lack leadership skills.

b) Introverts are inspirational leaders with high emotional intelligence.

c) Introverts are poor decision-makers.

d) Introverts avoid leadership roles.

8. What does the spectrum acknowledge?

a) Individuals are strictly introverted or extroverted.

b) Individuals exhibit varying degrees of introverted and extroverted characteristics.

c) Introversion and extroversion are irrelevant to personality.

d) Only extroverted traits are valuable in the workplace.

9. Which cultural attitude is associated with valuing introversion?

a) Individualist cultures.

b) Collectivist cultures.

c) Western cultures.

d) Corporate cultures.

10. What shift in behavior did Jake Thompson exhibit as he neared retirement?

a) From introverted to extroverted behaviors.

b) From extroverted to introverted behaviors.

c) From ambivert to introverted behaviors.

d) No change in behavior.

ANSWERS

Q1. b) Provide options for small-group discussions and let input come naturally.

Q2. a) Deep thinking, creativity, and attention to detail.

Q3. b) Analyze complex data and develop a detailed report independently.

Q4. b) 30-50%

Q5. c) Introverts are antisocial.

Q6. c) Reflective thinking.

Q7. b) Introverts are inspirational leaders with high emotional intelligence.

Q8. b) Individuals exhibit varying degrees of introverted and extroverted characteristics.

Q9. b) Collectivist cultures.

Q10. b) From extroverted to introverted behaviors.

ARE YOU AN
INTROVERT OR EXTROVERT?

Discover whether you are an introvert or an extrovert with this quick 8-question quiz. This is not a diagnosis, but a reflection tool.

1. How do you feel after attending a social event?

a) Energized and excited.

b) Drained and needing alone time.

2. When you need to recharge, what do you prefer?

a) Spending time with others.

b) Spending time alone.

3. In a group setting, do you usually:

a) Lead the conversation.

b) Listen more than you speak.

4. How do you prefer to communicate?

a) Verbally and in person.

b) Through writing or texting.

5. When faced with a problem, do you:

a) Seek advice from others.

b) Work through it independently.

6. Your ideal weekend would include:

a) Social activities and events.

b) Quiet, solitary activities.

7. In a new environment, are you more likely to:

a) Introduce yourself to new people immediately.

b) Observe and wait for others to approach you.

8. How do you handle interruptions while working?

a) Easily shift focus and welcome the break.

b) Find it disruptive and prefer to minimize it.

SCORING

MOSTLY A'S - YOU ARE AN EXTROVERT

You thrive on social interaction and external stimulation. Being around others energizes you, and you enjoy engaging in lively conversations.

MOSTLY B'S - YOU ARE AN INTROVERT

You feel most comfortable in quieter, more solitary environments. You need time to recharge and prefer deeper interactions over small talk.

MIXED A'S AND B'S - YOU ARE AN AMBIVERT

You display traits of introversion and extroversion, depending on the situation. You can enjoy social activities, but also value alone time to recharge.

EVERY VOICE MATTERS

CHAPTER 2
IMPORTANCE OF INCLUSIVITY

Introversion is a personality trait characterized by individuals who recharge in solitude. Unlike shyness and social anxiety, introversion reflects a preference for deep thinking and meaningful interactions.

Recognizing this distinction is crucial to unlock hidden potential and leverage the strengths of all employees.

It is not just a gesture toward diversity; it provides a strategic advantage. Introvert-friendly practices contribute to a more dynamic workplace culture.

Research suggests that half of the U.S. population identifies as introverts. Thus, thoughtful accommodations are essential. Stillness sparks action; brilliance brews in momentum.

ENHANCING EMPLOYEE WELL-BEING

Addressing hidden pressures and subtle energy debt can significantly reduce stressors and curb both job hopping and disengagement. The real burden isn't square footage; it's what people carry unseen.

A cubicle might be small, but the invisible weight of task masking is enormous.

Studies have shown that open office layouts can trigger focus fatigue and reduce effectiveness for introverted employees.

By mitigating these issues, organizations can preserve overall well-being and employee flow.

BOOSTING PRODUCTIVITY

Tailored workspaces with quiet areas can help introverts maintain micro-momentum and reduce the quiet climb of Boomerang Employees or the need for career cushioning in undervalued roles.

This environment led to innovative solutions, as introverts often excel in problem-solving positions. Steelcase found that 95% of workers value quiet and private spaces, but 31% lack access to such amenities.

Remember: Peace breeds progress; clarity drives change.

ALIGNING WITH BROADER VALUES

Workplaces that embrace diversity, equity, and inclusion promote ethical behavior, where employees are both fully invested and mobilized.

According to Gallup, companies with higher employee motivation experience 21% higher profitability and 17% higher productivity.

FOSTERING A MODERN WORKPLACE

As work settings evolve, virtual buffering, energy flex, and attention anchors are no longer options but a must-have.

Quietly Sparks underscores that celebrating introverts' inner strengths can significantly contribute to an organization's success. Sometimes, the quietest minds create the loudest impact.

This chapter also presents a real-world example of how managers can transform workplaces. The following story demonstrates how working styles enable introverts to thrive and contribute their best.

QUIET STRENGTH

TechVerse Solutions was renowned for its cutting-edge technology and relentless innovation. The office sprawled with collaborative zones and vibrant brainstorming areas.

Everywhere, the hum of creativity filled the air. And there was Maya, a gifted programmer who stood amid this energetic whirlwind.

Maya, in her early thirties, had a serene presence. She was of average height, with brown eyes and long, dark hair. It was usually tied back in a loose ponytail. Her desk had a small cactus and a picture of her family.

Her skills earned her a stellar academic career and a coveted position at TechVerse Solutions. Her mind was a finely tuned compass; others floundered in the fog.

However, her introverted tendencies created tension in this fast-paced culture. Boisterous brainstorming sessions and an open-plan setting presented significant barriers.

The vibrant office, once a symbol of innovation, had become a source of stress. She felt like an exiled angel, craving a shadowed corner to let her light breathe.

This disconnect culminated in a pivotal moment: Maya reached a breaking point. Mustering her courage, she approached her manager, Ali, a charismatic leader known for his progressive vision.

Ali was tall, with a commanding presence and an easy smile that put people at ease. His short, dark hair was always neatly styled, and he wore sharp, business-casual attire.

His background was as diverse as his team. He traveled extensively and worked in various sectors, bringing a wealth of experience and a deep understanding of different cultures.

Maya confided in Ali in his office, away from the constant buzz around. Her voice trembled as she spoke, but her message was clear:

"Ali, the current environment is detrimental to my productivity and well-being. The noise, the interruptions... I can't think. I can't work like this."

Ali listened intently and empathetically.

"Maya, I appreciate your honesty. I had no idea it was affecting you so badly. We need to address this for you and anyone who feels the same way," he replied.

Determined to address the issue, Ali spearheaded several initiatives. He introduced "*Hush Rooms*": distraction-free areas with soundproofing and ambient lighting.

Additionally, employees could choose whether to work from home or the office, based on what suits them best. Alternative communication channels, including asynchronous tools for brainstorming and feedback, were also created to reduce the dependency on real-time meetings.

The office shifted, like a tide turning in slow motion, each desk alive with the thrill of new horizons. Even the skeptics couldn't resist leaning in, caught off guard by possibilities they hadn't anticipated.

These changes were structural and cultural. Ali added workshops to educate the team about different working styles and the importance of accommodating preferences.

Ali ensured the successful implementation of his introvert-friendly strategy using a top-down approach. He verified that senior management endorsed his vision. Success depended on alignment and buy-in at every level.

By engaging the leadership team, he facilitated the adoption of innovative tactics throughout the company, leading to a cohesive and effective rollout of the new practices.

Maya felt a wave of relief as these changes occurred. The quiet zones became her sanctuary, where she flourished without interruption.

Freed from the pressure to adapt to a predominantly extroverted ideal, she developed a series of groundbreaking solutions that addressed complex issues in new and innovative ways.

One afternoon, Maya presented her latest project, an advanced algorithm that enhances data processing capabilities. Her soft voice filled the room as she explained intricate details. The room fell silent in awe as she concluded her speech.

"This is incredible, Maya," Ali said, breaking the silence. *"Your work is a game-changer."*

Her colleagues nodded in agreement, and a wave of applause followed. For the first time, Maya felt seen and valued. True genius whispers, but it moves mountains.

***

This is a testament to the importance of introverts, as they represent a significant portion of the workforce. Their unique abilities offer a powerful competitive advantage to organizations that look beyond stereotypes.

Companies debunk misconceptions, letting them act authentically instead of forcing them into an outdated, biased notion of *"cultural fit."*

Her story at TechVerse Solutions highlights the profound impact of the new practices. They affected job satisfaction, mental health, collaboration, and effectiveness.

As I have stated publicly, diversity is not optional, and inclusion is a force that cannot be ignored. Organizations are not immune to backlash, regardless of their size or stature.

Those that dismiss *"the others"* now face real reputational and financial consequences, as both consumers and investors are increasingly conscious of where they place their trust and their money.

In summary, fostering an introvert-friendly workplace is about embracing all forms of diversity and creating an environment where every employee can thrive. This approach unlocks remarkable outcomes and more harmonious, resilient, and innovative companies.

Ignorance carries no warning label…
until it backfires right under your nose.

CHAPTER 2 - QUIZ

This quiz assesses the understanding of key concepts covered in Chapter 2, which emphasizes the importance of creating an inclusive and supportive environment for introverted employees.

1. Why are introvert-friendly practices a true strategic advantage rather than a symbolic inclusion effort?

a) They reduce the need for leadership oversight.

b) They enhance engagement, productivity, and retention by reducing energy waste.

c) They primarily improve external employer branding.

d) They eliminate performance differences among employees.

2. What type of work environment is often preferred by introverts?

a) Open-plan offices with constant interaction.

b) Quiet spaces with minimal interruptions.

c) High-energy, collaborative workspaces.

d) Highly social and noisy environments.

3. How does accommodating introverted working styles most effectively strengthen team performance?

a) By minimizing collaboration.

b) By creating a balance between visibility and depth of contribution.

c) By prioritizing individual work over teamwork.

d) By reducing communication altogether.

4. What practice was introduced by Ali to support introverts at TechVerse Solutions?

a) Mandatory team-building activities.

b) Designated quiet zones and flexible work options.

c) Increased frequency of group meetings.

d) Regular social events and networking opportunities.

5. What problem do *Quiet Zones* primarily solve?

a) Limited opportunities for social engagement.

b) Energy depletion caused by constant stimulation and interruptions.

c) A lack of collaborative tools.

d) Insufficient performance monitoring.

6. What is one of the challenges of open-plan offices?

a) Lack of access to team meetings.

b) Excessive noise and frequent interruptions.

c) Limited access to project resources.

d) Overreliance on individual work.

7. How do flexible arrangements support sustained performance for introverted employees?

a) By reducing accountability.

b) By allowing alignment between energy cycles and work demands.

c) By eliminating the need for collaboration.

d) By increasing informal interactions.

8. Why is it important for senior management to endorse introvert-friendly strategies?

a) To comply with legal requirements.

b) To implement strategies uniformly across all levels.

c) To reduce costs associated with office redesign.

d) To increase the number of social events.

9. What impact did introvert-friendly practices have on Maya's work?

a) It made her less productive.

b) It increased stress and dissatisfaction.

c) It enabled her to develop innovative solutions and feel valued.

d) It resulted in her leaving the company.

10. Why does embracing different working styles strengthen organizational culture long-term?

a) It standardizes behavior across teams.

b) It reduces leadership responsibility.

c) It enables authentic contribution and sustainable engagement.

d) It limits creative tension.

ANSWERS

Q1. b) They enhance engagement, productivity, and retention by reducing energy waste.

Q2. b) Quiet spaces with minimal interruptions.

Q3. b) By creating a balance between visibility and depth of contribution.

Q4. b) Designated quiet zones and flexible work options.

Q5. b) Energy depletion caused by constant stimulation and interruptions.

Q6. b) Excessive noise and frequent interruptions.

Q7. b) By allowing alignment between energy cycles and work demands.

Q8. b) To implement strategies uniformly across all levels.

Q9. c) It enabled her to develop innovative solutions and feel valued.

Q10. c) It enables authentic contribution and sustainable engagement.

UNLOCKING HIDDEN POTENTIAL

CHAPTER 3

EMPOWERING

INTROVERTED EMPLOYEES

Workplaces are not neutral. For introverted employees, they can either sharpen productivity or quietly snap. When noise, urgency, and constant visibility rule by default, introverts are left navigating systems that reward volume over value.

Overstimulating environments, performative networking, and rapid-fire meetings drain energy rather than generate insight. The result is not immediate failure, but cumulative fatigue. When leadership ignores these dynamics, the consequences are real, even if delayed.

Empowerment begins with intention. Psychological safety allows professionals to work at their natural depth rather than on borrowed stamina.

This chapter explores the barriers they face, the risks of neglecting them, and the shifts that turn quiet capability into sustained contribution. Beneath still waters, minds are always plotting.

WARNING

Now, let's be real for a moment: I'm not here to scare you, make you bitter, or tell you to hate the system. I'm here to prepare you. Because once you understand how corporate *actually* works, you stop getting blindsided and playing small.

THE CORPORATE FAIRYTALE ENDS HERE

If you've ever wondered why you're stuck, overlooked, or overworked despite delivering results, this is your wake-up call.

Who gets promoted and who gets cut rarely aligns with merit alone. After too much polite nodding, it's time for accountability. HR can't continue acting as a lapdog to management while calling it *"people strategy."*

A NOTE TO INTROVERTS

This isn't just an HR problem. It's yours too. Waiting for leadership to notice you, or for HR to *"rewrite"* the playbook, will leave you standing still.

To climb the ladder and to shine, you need to understand the mechanics at play. And yes, the game isn't always fair.

But clarity about how things really operate gives you power that no one will ever hand you.

NOT FOR THE FAINT OF HEART

And for those still clinging to the illusion of fairness in the corporate world, let's get one thing straight…

HR manuals won't tell you this. Training seminars won't admit it. And your mentors probably won't either.

This next page reveals the truths no one dares to say out loud. If you're afraid of the real world behind the polished walls, turn back now…

But if you're ready to see what really lurks beneath the surface, keep reading.

WELCOME TO THE UNVARNISHED REALITY

Truth #1: Visibility Beats Performance For Promotions.

Truth #2: Your Job Is Replaceable. Build Your Brand.

Truth #3: Loyalty Won't Pay Your Bills.

Truth #4: Office Politics Aren't Optional.

Truth #5: Your Manager Is Not Your Friend or Family.

Truth #6: DEI Is PR.

Truth #7: Job Descriptions Are Fictional.

Truth #8: Most Meetings Are Useless.

Truth #9: Keep Your Ideas Safe.

Truth #10: The Perfect Workplace Doesn't Exist.

Truth #11: Networking Is Mandatory.

Truth #12: Job Security Is a Myth.

Truth #13: Money Runs Everything.

Truth #14: Corporate Is a Survival Game.

Truth #15: Your Career Is Your Responsibility.

For those brave enough to act, here is your blueprint on how introverts can claim influence, protect their energy, and secure a voice in the rooms that really matter.

CHALLENGES & RISKS

Amid constant motion and chatter, subtlety can slip under the radar; yet when noticed, it reshapes everything. Overlooking it isn't just careless; it's costly.

SENSORY OVERLOAD: Loud noises, bright lights, and crowded spaces aren't just annoying; they actively hinder focus. Studies show open-plan layouts can induce higher stress and lower productivity. Even routine networking events or office parties can trigger sensory fatigue, requiring time to recover.

NETWORKING & VISIBILITY: Career progression often favors those who are socially outgoing, making it harder for others to influence outcomes. Introverts may excel in meaningful interactions yet struggle in networking-heavy situations.

Truth #1 applies here and everywhere: Skipping events deemed useless or unnecessary can block even top performers from promotions.

MEETINGS & RAPID-FIRE COMMUNICATION: Quick brainstorming sessions and constant verbal input put introverts at a disadvantage. Processing internally takes time, and without it, their ideas can go unheard. Public speaking anxiety compounds the challenge, especially where talkativeness is equated with competence.

MISINTERPRETATION & MARGINALIZATION: A quieter demeanor is often mistaken for disengagement. Research shows introverts can feel undervalued, pressured to conform, and even alienated in extrovert-dominated workplaces.

CONSEQUENCES OF NEGLECT: Ignoring these dynamics has real costs: stress, burnout, diminished morale, and talent loss. Introverts may withdraw from discussions, limiting the organization's intellectual capital. High performers may attrit, taking valuable expertise with them.

UNTAPPED STRENGTHS: Dismissing their methods hampers innovation, compromises decisions, and disrupts operational alignment.

STRATEGIC RESPONSE: Flexible schedules, quiet zones, and the option to work remotely don't coddle introverts; they unlock their full capacity.

Ignoring subtle genius isn't humility, it's blindness.

THE ADVANTAGES OF AN INTROVERT-FRIENDLY WORKPLACE

Factoring introverts into policies isn't charity, it's vision. When quiet minds are empowered, the payoff is quantifiable, tangible, and sometimes surprising.

MENTAL CLARITY, NOT CHAOS

Providing spaces for uninterrupted focus isn't just about comfort; it's about unleashing intellectual horsepower. The result? Decisions are sharper, ideas are bolder, and mistakes shrink.

RETENTION & LOYALTY

Employees who feel respected stick around. Fewer departures mean preserved knowledge, stable teams, and reduced recruitment costs.

Turnover isn't just a number; it's a hidden drain on morale and the bottom line.

DEEP WORK EQUALS HIGH VALUE

They handle complex tasks with precision. Minimizing distractions doesn't just make them happier; it directly boosts quality and innovation breakthroughs.

BALANCED TEAMS, AMPLIFIED IDEAS

Projects move forward smoothly from plan to execution. This synergy isn't just collaboration, it's a supercharged payoff.

INTENTIONAL COMMUNICATION WINS

Authorizing written feedback and discussion isn't a nicety; it's a tactical advantage. Timely, considered input often surfaces solutions others miss in immediate verbal debate.

HIDDEN LEADERSHIP POTENTIAL

Where charisma dazzles but falters, introverted leaders prevail. Intentional, compassionate, perceptive, and steady, they forge sustainable leadership pipelines.

FLEXIBILITY IS FREEDOM

Remote options and adaptable schedules aren't perks; they're performance boosters. It converts effort management into real gains.

DIVERSITY IN PRACTICE, NOT JUST POLICY

Amplifying all voices isn't just fair, it's smart. Harnessing complementary strengths yields richer solutions and a culture that elevates reputation and brand credibility.

The takeaways are clear: implementing true workforce representation isn't just the right thing; it's a competitive edge.

Next, we'll see how physical spaces can make or break these advantages.

Smart leadership hears what silence has to say.

THE POWER OF DESIGN

The battle of the office layouts isn't just aesthetic. Open spaces promise collaboration, private offices offer focus, and hybrid models dare to do both. But the real winners are organizations that understand the subtle psychology behind it and harness it to boost performance and retention.

OPEN OFFICES

The Social Playground... With A Catch

Spontaneous conversations spark new ideas. Proximity builds camaraderie. And managers can keep an eye on the team without playing hide-and-seek.

Studies show open spaces can increase teamwork by 20% and reduce real estate costs by up to 30%.

Sounds perfect, right? Not so fast...

Noise levels spike. Privacy shrinks. Deep thinking gets derailed. Employees in open offices report 25% drops in focus and frequent distractions, turning potential energy into mental static.

Open layouts reward the talkative, but at what cost?

PRIVATE OFFICES

Focused Power With Tradeoffs

Quiet, controlled, and customizable offices are the ideal haven for introverts. Errors drop, and satisfaction jumps by 20 to 30%. When concentration is king, they reign supreme.

So far, so good… but there's a trap: isolation.

Physical walls can block collaboration and spontaneousness by 15%, and even stunt face-to-face communication.

Private offices aren't one-size-fits-all. Paired them with meeting hubs, lounges, or shared *"touchdown"* areas to keep team cohesion.

HYBRID AND ADAPTIVE WORKSPACES

The Goldilocks Zone

The future isn't open *or* private, it's adaptive. Salesforce, for example, merges communal hub with silent nooks, boosting satisfaction by 20%.

Adaptive spaces give employees the freedom to choose how they work. Flexibility isn't just convenient, it's transformational.

Remote options and adjustable schedules let employees manage their energy, protect their creativity, and prevent burnout. This balance is a revenue multiplier.

THE DILEMMA

Space vs. Human Behavior

No layout is flawless. It can invigorate, alienate, or exhaust. The key is designing environments with a range of options employees can select to maximize output.

TANGIBLE BENEFITS:

- *Quiet Zones:* 48% better concentration, 29% boost in creative problem-solving, 35% higher satisfaction.

- *Flexible Work:* 77% improved work-life balance, 20% lower turnover, 13% higher remote productivity.

- *Alternative Channels:* 25% more participation, 40% better collaborative efficiency, 17% higher engagement.

THE LESSON: Setting up office space isn't decoration. It amplifies talent and safeguards well-being into organizational advantage. It isn't just about rules or policies; it's about reinventing an ecosystem where workflows converge. This is where architecture meets human potential, setting the stage for the next chapter: *Inclusivity as a Strategic Imperative.*

INCLUSION AS ADVANTAGE

CHAPTER 4
INCLUSIVITY AS A STRATEGIC IMPERATIVE

Quiet contributions are no longer optional; they're a competitive edge. In today's workforce, employees and investors alike expect more than slogans. Diversity isn't a PR move anymore; performative gestures are detected instantly, and backlash hits hard financially, reputationally, and legally.

Organizations that treat inclusion as a branding exercise rather than a genuine business function risk eroding trust, losing talent, and undermining their credibility.

"If your DEI strategy looks good on LinkedIn but feels hollow at the water cooler, it's time for a reality check. Employees see through performative diversity, and the gap between what companies say and what they tolerate internally becomes impossible to hide."

True inclusivity aligns actions with values, ensures policies translate into lived experiences, and builds resilience against missteps. Companies that embed this mindset don't just retain talent, they attract it, convert it into engagement, and unlock measurable advantage.

The question isn't whether introverts or any underrepresented voices should adapt. The question is whether your organization can adapt to them.

Let's move past "*cultural fit*" and demand cultural "*contribution.*" Those who get it don't just survive; they set the pace.

ACTIVATION PLAYBOOK

Top talent doesn't announce itself, but overlooking it comes at a cost. This section explores how organizations move beyond symbolism to translate wishful proposals into reality. Grounded in case studies, it provides actionable examples to adopt and scale.

Awareness is the briefing. Execution is the decision. And leadership is revealed not by what's acknowledged, but by what's acted on.

WORKSHOPS THAT ACTUALLY STICK

Awareness isn't taught once;
It's reinforced until assumptions lose their grip.

Case Study: A large technology company held quarterly workshops on personality dynamics. Following these sessions, employees reported a 30% increase in understanding and consideration of quieter working styles. The result was stronger alignment across teams and a measurable lift in overall output.

LEAD BY LISTENING

When leaders name themselves, others stop hiding.

Case Study: At a financial services firm, the CEO openly shared his experience navigating leadership as a reserved professional. This visibility normalized alternative leadership styles and prompted senior managers to adopt more deliberate, people-aware approaches.

ONBOARDING WITH INSIGHT

Culture isn't taught; It's absorbed.

Case Study: A marketing agency redesigned its onboarding experience to include education on different working styles. New hires reported smoother integration, clearer expectations, and stronger early engagement with peers across the organization.

FLEXIBILITY THAT COUNTS

Flexibility isn't generosity; It's a retention strategy.

Case Study: A software development firm introduced employee-selected remote and in-office options. Those who chose quieter settings reported sustained output, contributing to a 20% reduction in turnover.

SPACES THAT EMPOWER

Space sends signals long before policies do.

Case Study: An architectural firm incorporated additional low-stimulation zones into its office design. Employees using these spaces reported a 25% improvement in task completion efficiency, particularly on complex assignments.

TALK LESS, SHARE MORE

Not every idea arrives at full volume.

Case Study: A healthcare organization revised its communication norms to prioritize written updates and asynchronous input. Participation broadened noticeably, resulting in more balanced knowledge exchange and a 15% rise in viable solution proposals.

SAFE SPACES TO SPEAK UP

Silence isn't disengagement if you know how to listen.

Case Study: An international NGO launched monthly *"Working Style Forums"* where employees discussed preferences and friction points. These conversations strengthened mutual respect and reduced misinterpretation across departments.

GUIDED GROWTH PATHS

Talent grows faster when it isn't forced to self-explain.

Case Study: A law firm introduced a mentorship program pairing junior professionals with senior leaders who shared similar working styles. Participants reported clearer career navigation and stronger long-term confidence in their progression.

CELEBRATING EVERY VOICE

What gets celebrated decides what gets repeated.

Case Study: A multinational organization launched a *"Diversity of Thought"* initiative spotlighting varied contribution styles. By reshaping internal success narratives, the company reinforced legitimacy and fairness.

***

Awareness alone changes nothing. What matters is what gets embedded into daily practice.

The examples above show how organizations move from acknowledgment to execution, hardwiring space for quieter contributions to shape decisions that matter.

When this shift is done right, performance stabilizes, trust deepens, and momentum compounds.

Next, we turn to what happens beyond programs and policies: how presence is claimed, credibility is protected, and careers are advanced inside systems that were never built with neutrality in mind.

UNMUTING TALENT

Inclusive communication isn't about being polite or complaisant. It's about eliminating the structural noise that prevents insight from traveling upward, outward, and into decisions. When the expression is frictionless, the contribution scales.

MAKE INFORMATION LAND

If clarity feels uncomfortable, it's usually because power was hiding in ambiguity.

Clear language isn't simplification; it's precision. When messages are stripped of jargon, excess urgency, and performative complexity, comprehension rises, and costly errors fall.

MULTIPLY ENTRY POINTS

Ideas don't need louder rooms; they need more doors.

Not every idea arrives through spontaneous debate. Offering multiple channels: written updates, digital platforms, and asynchronous tools. It ensures insight isn't filtered by speed or volume.

SIGNAL THAT INPUT MATTERS

Being heard isn't emotional; It's operational.

Collection without response breeds silence. When leaders visibly acknowledge, act on, or revisit employee input, expression becomes worth the effort.

CREATE SAFE EXCHANGE ZONES

Psychological safety isn't softness; It's signal integrity.

Open dialogue doesn't emerge by accident. Structured forums give employees permission to surface differences without reputational risk.

ADAPT TO CONTEXT, NOT AVERAGES

Equity starts where assumptions end.

Communication systems fail when they assume uniform needs. Flexibility, especially in terms of accessibility and cultural nuance, helps retain talent from disengaging quietly.

AUDIT WHAT ACTUALLY WORKS

What isn't reviewed slowly breaks.

Inclusive communication isn't set-and-forget. Feedback loops, surveys, and iteration ensure systems evolve instead of fossilizing.

Without attention, even the clearest channels calcify. Momentum dies where oversight stops. When friction is removed, contribution becomes consistent, trust compounds, and decisions improve.

This isn't about saying more. It's about making sure the right things get through.

DEI isn't a checklist; It's infrastructure.

CALIBRATING LEADERSHIP POWER

Leadership isn't about being the loudest voice in the room; it's about how authority is exercised. Systems often reward visibility, but real impact comes from measured action, thoughtful timing, and creating space for ideas to emerge. Quiet leaders shape outcomes by leveraging presence rather than dominating it.

LEVERAGING AUTHORITY

Introverted leaders excel at pacing input, listening before acting, and turning reflection into strategy. By allowing authority to unfold methodically, organizations benefit from more deliberate, less reactive decisions.

As one CEO put it, *"Power doesn't need a microphone; it needs a compass."*

CHALLENGING PRESUMPTIONS

Most leadership frameworks favor extroverted energy. Recalibrating authority to value insight over immediacy unlocks perspectives that are often invisible in high-decibel environments. Success isn't about constant visibility; it's about timing, perspective, and restraint.

STRUCTURING DECISION FLOW

Slow the cascade, broaden the lens. Introducing deliberate pauses, written inputs, and small-group deliberations ensures ideas aren't drowned out by speed or social volume. Quality rises when authority respects reflection.

ACCESSIBLE LEADERSHIP

Being approachable is tactical, not just nice. When systems encourage leaders to be reachable without performative gestures, employees engage more honestly. Accessibility fosters trust and improves alignment across teams.

FOSTERING SYSTEMIC FLEXIBILITY

Leadership effectiveness grows when rules around input, feedback, and escalation adapt to diverse cognitive and social styles. Policies that accommodate asynchronous contribution and thoughtful debate amplify the organization's intelligence without privileging talkers over thinkers.

THE QUIET MULTIPLIER

When authority is calibrated to reward thoughtfulness over impulse, organizations gain precision, foresight, and resilience. Quiet leadership transforms the flow of decisions, creating a workplace where all talents, silent or outspoken, can move the needle.

Understanding how systems shape outcomes is only half the battle. The next step is testing your grasp of practical approaches that make workplaces truly introvert-friendly.

In the upcoming quiz, you'll see how well you can spot opportunities, apply strategies, and recognize subtle levers that turn insight into action.

CHAPTER 4 - QUIZ

Welcome to the quiz on *Inclusivity as a Strategic Imperative*. Let's determine how well you understand introvert-friendly practical approaches.

1. **True or False:** Diversity initiatives succeed even if employees sense they are performative.

2. **What distinguishes *"cultural contribution"* from *"cultural fit"*?**
a) Matching personalities.
b) Shaping and improving culture actively.
c) Adapting quietly to existing norms.
d) Focusing on senior leadership preferences.

3. **Which action best moves inclusion from awareness to execution?**
a) Holding a single diversity workshop.
b) Embedding policies into daily practices.
c) Celebrating achievements only externally.
d) Issuing one-time surveys.

4. **Why is flexible work considered a strategic tool?**
a) Reduces meeting times.

b) Boosts retention and engagement.

c) Replaces leadership training.

d) Improves office décor.

5. How can organizations amplify quieter voices effectively?

a) Require verbal contributions in every meeting.

b) Provide multiple ways to share ideas.

c) Limit asynchronous communication.

d) Reward visibility over insight.

6. True or False: Psychological safety naturally emerges without structured forums.

7. The "*Quiet Multiplier*" principle emphasizes:

a) Loudness equals influence.

b) Insight drives better outcomes.

c) Constant visibility is critical.

d) Speed over accuracy.

8. Which leadership behavior fosters trust and honest engagement?

a) Rewarding rapid decisions only.

b) Creating space for reflection and structured input.

c) Prioritizing extroverted employees.

d) Avoiding feedback mechanisms.

9. **True or False:** Clear, precise communication reduces errors and ensures contributions are understood.

10. **What's the key risk of treating DEI as a branding exercise?**

a) Faster decision-making.

b) Loss of credibility, trust, and talent.

c) Improved product innovation.

d) Reduced administrative burden.

ANSWERS

Q1. False.

Q2. b) Shaping and improving culture actively.

Q3. b) Embedding policies into daily practices.

Q4. b) Boosts retention and engagement.

Q5. b) Provide multiple ways to share ideas.

Q6. False.

Q7. b) Insight drives better outcomes.

Q8. b) Creating space for reflection and structured input.

Q9. True.

Q10. b) Loss of credibility, trust, and talent.

REFRAMING LEARNING

CHAPTER 5
TRAINING FOR EMPLOYEE
UNDERSTANDING

In today's workplace, the ability to pause, reflect, and regulate one's internal state drives far more than morale; it steers decisions, leadership quality, and organizational resilience.

Training programs rooted in introspection don't slow companies down; they prevent them from bleeding energy through misalignment, conflict, and avoidable burnout.

Introspective training sharpens employees' responses under pressure. It teaches professionals to recognize their internal signals before those signals quietly sabotage collaboration, judgment, or retention.

For introverted employees in particular, introspection isn't an abstract exercise; it's a native operating system. When organizations legitimize reflective work rather than forcing constant outward performance, they unlock precision, emotional intelligence, and sustainable output.

Empathy is no longer a soft skill…

… It's a performance driver.

Below is a focused overview of why introspective training delivers measurable impact, supported by real-world examples that move this conversation beyond theory.

REFLECTIVE GROWTH

Decision-Making Starts Internally

Introspective training strengthens emotional intelligence not as self-help, but as decision infrastructure. Employees who understand their internal reactions make fewer reactive choices, communicate with clarity, and lead without unnecessary friction. Reflection didn't make them slower. It made them sharper.

TEAM SYNERGY

Awareness Changes Behavior

Teams don't fracture because people lack skills. It occurs when people underestimate their impact on others. This approach forces that awareness into focus. When employees see how their assumptions shift perspectives and spark action, teamwork stops being accidental and becomes intentional.

Alignment didn't spring from sameness. It honors differences.

STRESS MANAGEMENT

Stop Leaking Energy

Unchecked stress doesn't just exhaust employees; it quietly erodes judgment, adaptability, and output. Such techniques equip employees to identify stress signals early and respond strategically, not reactively.

Stress didn't disappear. But it stopped running the system.

CONFLICT RESOLUTION

When Friction Becomes Data

Conflict is not a breakdown of culture; it's feedback. The real failure occurs when teams lack the internal discipline to interpret it. This method reframes conflict as a signal rather than a threat.

Employees pause and examine their reactions with maturity instead of defensiveness. The result is not avoidance, but precision: issues surface earlier, conversations become clearer, and resolutions last longer.

The goal isn't harmony; It's clarity.

SELF-DEVELOPMENT

Ownership Changes Trajectory

Most programs fail because they outsource responsibility. Participants sit passively, hoping someone else will fix their blind spots. Results are temporary, at best.

These practices flip the script. It hands the reins back to the individual. Growth becomes deliberate. Change sticks. Ownership fuels progress.

When employees understand how their patterns, limits, and strengths shape outcomes, development stops being aspirational and becomes deliberate.

Growth is no longer tied to titles or timelines, but to informed choices. Progress stopped being assigned. It became conscious.

CASE STUDY: WHEN SPACE CHANGES PERFORMANCE

To further illustrate the profound impact of this training, consider the testimony of Jenna, a team leader. Her journey through introspective discovery reveals how it transformed her management approach.

BEFORE INTROSPECTIVE TRAINING

Jenna, a mid-level manager at a growing startup, struggled to balance a web of personalities and conflicting priorities. She was juggling sparks in a storm, with each team member threatening to ignite chaos.

DURING THE TRAINING

Jenna participated in workshops. Through these sessions, she gained valuable insights into her stress triggers and learned effective managerial strategies. She began to see patterns she hadn't noticed before.

DEVELOPMENT OF EMPATHY

Additionally, Jenna developed a heightened sense of empathy, giving her the lens to spot issues early and guide her team toward smoother leadership.

IMPACT AND RESULTS

The change was palpable. Jenna's improved communication and stress management led to a more cohesive and motivated crew.

Meetings flowed, tensions eased, and the office felt less like a pressure cooker and more like a launchpad for ideas.

Her journey proved that transformation isn't a program; it's a practice that spreads softly but reshapes everything it touches.

Introspective training only creates value when it is embedded, not appended. Organizations that succeed don't treat reflection as a standalone workshop or a once-a-year initiative; they integrate it into how people work, lead, and evaluate progress.

When introspection becomes operational, it shifts from a personal exercise to an organizational advantage.

Effective implementation includes:

- Structured reflection prompts embedded into workflows, not added as optional extras.

- Manager training that treats processing time as productivity, not hesitation.

- Performance frameworks that recognize depth, judgment, and signal detection, not just visibility.

This is where most companies fail. They introduce reflection without changing systems, and then wonder why nothing moves.

When introspection is no longer optional, it produces results. This isn't about slowing down culture. It's about removing wasted motion.

RESOURCEFUL ARSENAL

Nowadays, employers must integrate tools and programs that accommodate diverse working styles. These resources answer the requirements of introverted employees.

COMMUNICATION TOOLS

Let employees engage on their own terms.

- Slack: Respond thoughtfully, without the pressure of immediate replies.
- Microsoft Teams: Blend live conversations with delayed responses for flexibility.
- Basecamp: Structured updates keep information flowing without nonstop meetings.

PROJECT MANAGEMENT

Make work visible without constant interruptions.

- Trello: Visual boards help individuals plan and contribute at their own rhythm.
- Asana: Track timelines and progress clearly, reducing the need for check-ins.
- Monday.com: Adaptable workflows let employees work in the style that suits them best.

COLLABORATION PLATFORMS

Encourage participation without requiring verbal dominance.

- Miro & Mural: Visual boards allow idea-sharing and brainstorming without raising your voice.

FOCUS AND MINDFULNESS

Create environments where concentration thrives.

- Headspace: Mindfulness exercises to reset and recharge.
- Noisli: Customizable background sound improves focus without distraction.

FEEDBACK AND INSIGHT

Capture perspectives safely and honestly.

- SurveyMonkey & Officevibe: Let employees contribute input privately, promoting candor and engagement.

ACCESSIBILITY AND WRITING SUPPORT

Streamline expression and reduce misunderstandings.

- TextExpander: Simplifies repetitive tasks and messages.

- Grammarly: Clarifies writing, ensuring ideas land clearly.

LEARNING AND DEVELOPMENT

Turn awareness into action.

- Diversity & Inclusion Courses: LinkedIn Learning and Coursera.
- Communication Skills: Center for Creative Leadership and Dale Carnegie.
- Introversion Awareness: The Introverted Edge and Quiet Revolution.
- Leadership Growth: Harvard Business School Online and Korn Ferry.
- Wellness & Resilience: MBSR and Mental Health First Aid.

ADDITIONAL STRATEGIES

Bridge knowledge and real-world application.

- Mentorship Programs: Match employees with mentors who understand their background.
- Structured Feedback *Channels:* Encourage open dialogue without pressure.

Resources alone aren't enough...

Their power comes to life when integrated into daily workflows, leadership practices, and performance frameworks.

Reflection stops being optional and starts producing measurable results, turning introspection into a competitive advantage rather than a soft skill.

CHAPTER 5 - QUIZ

This quiz reinforces the concepts from Chapter 5 by encouraging reflection on personal experiences and perspectives. Test your inner knowledge!

1. What is the impact of reflective training on employee satisfaction?

a) Increased employee turnover by 30%.

b) Decreased productivity by 20%.

c) Improved employee satisfaction by 30%.

d) Reduced communication effectiveness by 15%.

2. How did introspective training affect team cohesion at the consulting firm?

a) Team cohesion decreased by 10%.

b) Team cohesion increased by 20%.

c) Had no impact on team cohesion.

d) Led to more frequent conflicts.

3. What percentage improvement in stress management was reported by the financial service company after introspective training?

a) 10%

b) 25%

c) 40%

d) 15%

4. What is the benefit of training for conflict resolution?

a) Increased number of internal disputes.

b) Decreased conflict resolution effectiveness.

c) Significant drop in internal disputes.

d) No change in conflict resolution.

5. What improvement did the retail chain observe in employee engagement and development after implementing introspective training?

a) 10% increase.

b) 20% increase.

c) 15% increase.

d) 5% increase.

6. How did training help Jenna?

a) Increased her stress levels.

b) Led to more conflicts with her team.

c) Improved her communication and stress management.

d) Reduced her ability to address inclusivity issues.

7. Which tool is designed to provide guided meditations and mindfulness exercises to manage workplace stress?

a) Noisli.

b) Grammarly.

c) Headspace.

d) SurveyMonkey.

8. What type of training does the *"Quiet Revolution"* program focus on?

a) Enhancing leadership skills.

b) Managing workplace stress.

c) Understanding and supporting introverts.

d) Improving project management.

9. Which software tool is used for visual collaboration and online brainstorming?

a) Basecamp.

b) Miro.

c) Asana.

d) Microsoft Teams.

10. What outcome did the software company expect after implementing regular feedback sessions?

a) Decreased employee morale.

b) Improved communication effectiveness.

c) Increased turnover rates.

d) Reduced team productivity.

ANSWERS

Q1. c) Improved employee satisfaction by 30%.

Q2. b) Team cohesion increased by 20%.

Q3. b) 25%.

Q4. c) Significant drop in internal disputes.

Q5. c) 15% increase.

Q6. c) Improved her communication and stress management.

Q7. c) Headspace.

Q8. c) Understanding and supporting introverts.

Q9. b) Miro.

Q10. b) Improved communication effectiveness.

BEYOND THE SPOTLIGHT

CHAPTER 6
INTERVIEW OF TOP TALENTS

In a competitive landscape, organizations are seeking a range of capabilities. Yet default hiring formats, especially high-pressure video calls with cameras on, often favor extroverts, leaving quieter candidates overlooked.

Take Mia, for example: she aced a written skills assessment but froze on a group live panel, and she went unnoticed.

It's time to rethink how we assess talent to ensure introverts have an equal chance to shine.

INTERVIEW-SPECIFIC FOCUS

Real-time evaluations reward speed and verbal dominance. By integrating written, scenario-based, and reflective tests, organizations can uncover the potential of introverted talent that might otherwise be missed.

INTERVIEW CONTEXT

Introverted candidates often give their best when given time to reflect and respond. The setting itself can either mimic or obstruct their natural strengths, so asynchronous questions can reveal insights that a high-pressure interrogation might obscure.

INTERVIEW OUTCOME

Outcome equity depends on how assessment criteria are designed and implemented. A thoughtfully designed process signals that all voices are represented and valued.

ACTIONABLE GUIDANCE

Bias emerges when interviews prioritize speed, verbal fluency, or manufactured energy. Introducing pacing, reflection windows, and alternative response channels levels the playing field and gives introverts an equitable opportunity to demonstrate their capabilities.

These shifts recalibrate hiring decisions toward capability rather than performance style.

NEW VISIONS

Hiring decisions are only as good as the cues an interview is supposed to capture. When evaluation relies on speed, visibility, or first impressions, it doesn't reveal capability; it filters for temperament.

The following shifts recalibrate interviews to surface substance, not showmanship.

RECOGNIZING DEPTH

Some candidates think before they speak. Others refine ideas internally before sharing them. Interviews that reward immediacy often miss this depth entirely.

Designing questions that probe reasoning, judgment, and decision logic, rather than verbal agility, reveals competence that standard formats overlook.

IMPLEMENTING WRITTEN EVALUATION

Written exercises don't dilute rigor; they sharpen it. Case responses, take-home analyses, or scenario breakdowns reveal how candidates structure their thoughts, prioritize information, and solve problems when pressure is removed. This isn't accommodation but clarity.

PRIORITIZING ONE-ON-ONE EXCHANGE

Group interviews amplify social dynamics. One-on-one conversations allow candidates to articulate their thinking without competing for airtime. The result is a richer explanation, clearer evidence, and fewer false negatives driven by room dynamics rather than ability.

REFOCUSING BEHAVIORAL QUESTIONS

Questions centered on personal decision points, not collective anecdotes, produce cleaner data. Asking how a candidate identified a risk, navigated ambiguity, or corrected a misstep surfaces ownership, discernment, and accountability without relying on storytelling.

DIVERSIFYING INTERVIEW MODES

A single format captures a narrow slice of talent. Offering alternatives, live discussions, delayed responses, or scenario follow-up reduces distortion caused by nerves, speed bias, or artificial urgency. What changes is not the standard, but the accuracy.

USING JOB LISTINGS AS FILTERS

Candidates self-select based on what a role signals. Job descriptions with clear outcomes, autonomy, and evaluation criteria attract applicants aligned with substance over spectacle. This sets expectations before the first conversation begins.

MAKING SUCCESS VISIBLE

Highlighting varied paths to impact reframes what "*high performance*" looks like. When organizations showcase achievement rooted in judgment, consistency, and depth, candidates understand that contribution, not volume, earns credibility.

Real-World Winner: Innovatech revamped interviews. Quiet candidates who once vanished in panels now rose to the top. One analyst boosted client retention 22% without saying a word live. Brilliance doesn't shout; it delivers.

RETHINKING NETWORKING TOUCHPOINTS

Smaller, focused interactions outperform crowded events. With targeted conversations, candidates ask meaningful questions and assess fit without navigating environments that reward presence over perception.

CLARIFYING THE PROCESS

Uncertainty distorts merit. Outlining interview stages, evaluation methods, and decision timelines improves preparation quality and reduces noise caused by guesswork. Precision invites precision.

CLOSING THE LOOP

Candidate feedback is diagnostic, not decorative. Reviewing where strong applicants disengage or underperform reveals flaws in the process itself. Continuous calibration improves selection integrity over time.

When interviews are designed to extract insight instead of energy, hiring outcomes improve. The goal isn't to favor one personality over another; it's to distinguish between visibility and value.

INTERVIEWER GUIDELINES

The goal of an interview is not to test confidence under artificial pressure, but to check how a candidate prioritizes and operates when the noise is removed. These questions should reveal depth, judgment, and mindset, without rewarding a fake act for performance's sake.

WORK STYLE & CONDITIONS
FOR EXCELLENCE

1. Under what conditions do you consistently produce your best work, and what tends to degrade the quality of your output? *(Reveals self-awareness and performance boundaries.)*

2. Describe a work environment where your impact was strongest. What specifically enabled that? *(Focuses on systems, not preferences.)*

3. When a role requires sustained effort over time, how do you maintain momentum without burnout? *(Signals endurance strategy, not motivation slogans.)*

4. What type of feedback materially improves your performance, and what type tends to be unhelpful? Why? *(Tests discernment, not sensitivity.)*

COMMUNICATION & COLLABORATION

1. How do you prepare when you know a discussion will influence decisions rather than just exchange updates? *(Surface preparation discipline.)*

2. Walk me through a situation where you had to translate a complex idea for people with very different levels of context. *(Tests clarity, not charisma.)*

3. When working with colleagues whose styles differ sharply from yours, what do you adjust, and what do you not compromise on? *(Reveals adaptability with boundaries.)*

4. In group settings, how do you ensure your thinking is represented even when the discussion moves quickly? *(Shows strategic participation.)*

PROBLEM-SOLVING & DECISION QUALITY

1. Tell me about a problem where the obvious solution was wrong. How did you recognize that? *(Elite signal: judgment over instinct.)*

2. When faced with incomplete information, what determines whether you wait, investigate, or act? *(Reveals decision thresholds.)*

3. Describe a time when collaboration improved your decision, and a time when it diluted it. *(Nuanced understanding of teamwork.)*

ENERGY, PRESSURE & SUSTAINABILITY

1. How do you detect early signs that pressure is beginning to affect your decision quality? *(Indicates internal calibration.)*

2. What practices help you recover focus after periods of sustained intensity? *(Tests sustainability, not resilience clichés.)*

3. Which work arrangement has historically produced your highest-quality outcomes, and why? *(Anchors flexibility to results.)*

GROWTH, RANGE & ADAPTABILITY

1. Describe a professional situation that initially felt misaligned with your natural style. How did you navigate it? *(Growth without forcing extroversion.)*

2. How do you keep your thinking current without chasing every new trend? *(Separates depth from noise.)*

Avoid scoring candidates on speed, volume, or immediacy:

- Structure of thought

- Precision of language

- Ability to reflect and correct

- Evidence of judgment under ambiguity

Strong candidates may pause. That pause is data.

Time to see if you spot talent where others only see noise. Let's put it to the test.

CHAPTER 6 - QUIZ

Can you tell substance from showmanship? Answer these 5 scenarios and prove your hiring radar is tuned to depth, not volume.

1. You're interviewing a candidate who pauses before answering. Do you:

a) Rush them to keep the panel moving.

b) Note the pause as a sign of careful thought.

c) Penalize them for being slow.

2. A candidate aces a written case but struggles in a high-pressure video panel. What's the best takeaway?

a) They aren't ready for the role.

b) Their potential may be hidden by format bias.

c) They need extroversion coaching.

3. When designing an interview, which element most reduces bias against introverts?

a) Speed-focused live Q&A.

b) Asynchronous or scenario-based tasks.

c) Group icebreakers.

4. If your team celebrates *"volume over value"* in networking events, what might you miss?

a) Quiet innovators with breakthrough ideas.

b) People are good at small talk.

c) Team synergy.

5. Which metric should matter most when evaluating candidates?

a) First impression charisma.

b) Depth of reasoning and clarity of thought.

c) Number of times they speak.

ANSWERS: Q1-b ; Q2-b ; Q3-b ; Q4-a ; Q5-b.

ENERGY THAT LAST

CHAPTER 7
MENTAL HEALTH
BURNOUT AND STRESS

Workplace exhaustion is no longer anecdotal. According to the American Psychological Association, 61% of employees report feeling chronically overwhelmed by work demands. This strain is not evenly distributed.

For introverts who represent more than half of the U.S. workforce, the modern workplace introduces additional points of friction that quietly compound fatigue and disengagement.

Most Western office environments reward visibility, immediacy, and constant interaction. Assertiveness is interpreted as competence. Presence is mistaken for contribution.

For employees who restore energy through solitude and concentration, open-plan offices, persistent collaboration, and uninterrupted social exposure act less like enablers and more like erosion. The issue is not temperament; it is environmental mismatch.

Research supports this distinction. A Harvard Business Review analysis found that introverted employees are 30% more likely to experience anxiety tied directly to workplace design settings that conflict with how they process information, recover focus, and perform at their best.

When the environment consistently demands outward energy, inward thinkers pay the cost.

This cost is often invisible until it manifests as a withdrawal, reduced engagement, or attrition. A survey reported that 50% of introverted employees felt undervalued, not because their output was lacking, but because their contributions were less visible in systems calibrated for speed and volume rather than depth and judgment.

What reduces this friction is not surface-level accommodation, but structural recalibration:

- Autonomy over location and timing reduces unnecessary cognitive drain.

  Stanford research shows that distributed work models improve output by 13%, largely by removing interference rather than increasing effort.

- Asynchronous communication channels allow ideas to be evaluated on clarity rather than immediacy. Studies in the *Journal of Business Psychology* indicate that introverted professionals perform more effectively when given time to process and respond.

- Private, specific feedback loops sharpen performance more reliably than public recognition. Gallup data shows that individualized feedback increases engagement among introverted employees by 57%.

- Team literacy around cognitive diversity reduces the misinterpretation of quietness as disengagement. The Center for Creative Leadership links this awareness to higher satisfaction and lower attrition.

- Boundaries around work intensity and recovery correlate with measurable reductions in strain. World Health Organization data associates adaptive scheduling models with a 25% decrease in reported overload.

- Emotional acuity at the managerial level determines whether pressure escalates or stabilizes.

Leaders who can read depletion signals early prevent silent performance decay.

The takeaway is not that individuals need to *"cope better,"* but that organizations must design work that does not steadily drain a large portion of their talent.

When systems applaud constant output signals over sustained cognitive contribution, depletion is not a personal failure; it is a predictable outcome of the design.

ANTI-BURNOUT STRATEGIES

Sustained performance is not a matter of resilience; it is a matter of design. When output steadily declines across teams, the issue is rarely motivation. It is a signal overload, recovery debt, and a poorly governed effort.

High-functioning organizations treat human capacity as a finite asset measured, protected, and renewed with intent.

The most effective interventions do not attempt to energize people. They remove the conditions that drain them in the first place.

COGNITIVE REGULATION PRACTICES

Attention is the scarcest resource in modern work. Techniques such as guided focus training, controlled breathing, and cognitive reframing are not wellness trends; they are performance tools.

Google's *Search Inside Yourself* initiative demonstrated significant reductions in reported overload and measurable gains in emotional regulation and clarity. The value lies not in calm, but in decision quality under pressure.

WORKLOAD ARCHITECTURE

Output improves when effort is bounded. Stanford research showed that reducing excessive hours led to a 13% increase in productivity, largely because fewer hours eliminated diminishing returns.

Precision beats endurance.
Clear priorities and realistic pacing protect judgment.

CONFIDENTIAL INTERVENTION CHANNELS

When personal strain spills into performance, discretion matters. Access to confidential counseling and advisory services enables employees to course-correct before issues surface as absenteeism or disengagement.

Data from the Employee Assistance Professional Association links these services to lower absence rates and higher job satisfaction. Early intervention preserves continuity.

PHYSICAL CAPACITY AS
A PERFORMANCE MULTIPLIER

Sustained cognitive output depends on physical health. Johnson & Johnson's long-standing investment in employee health initiatives yielded a documented return of $2.71 for every dollar spent, driven by reduced medical costs and improved productivity. Depleted bodies produce compromised thinking.

RECOVERY GOVERNANCE

Continuous effort without interruption degrades accuracy. The American Psychological Association found that employees who took regular breaks demonstrated higher productivity and lower cognitive fatigue.

Rest is not an absence of work; It is a prerequisite for sustained precision.

TASK CONTROL AND TIME LITERACY

When people lack control over task sequencing, they task mask, surviving. Training in workload planning and prioritization equips employees to protect focus and manage complexity.

The Project Management Institute reports substantial reductions in reported overload following structured time-management training. Control restores clarity.

STRUCTURAL OPTIONALITY

Retention improves when roles allow adaptation to life constraints without penalty. SHRM data shows that employees with adaptive scheduling options are more likely to remain with their employer. The benefit is not convenience; it is continuity of expertise.

The objective is not to make work easier. It is to make performance sustainable. Organizations that preserve capacity outperform those that repeatedly extract it.

What appears to be care on the surface is, at its core, disciplined operational intelligence.

COGNITIVE SUSTAINABILITY

Rules don't just dictate behavior; they sculpt the flow of thought, decision-making, and performance. Strong governance creates conditions where focus sharpens, judgment thrives, and talent flourishes.

CRYSTAL-CLEAR EXPECTATIONS

Ambiguity is the enemy of output. Define deliverables and priorities so energy is invested in value, not guesswork.

ALIGNMENT INTERACTIONS

Regular touchpoints keep objectives synced and friction minimal, ensuring small misalignments don't compound into major disruptions.

MEANINGFUL RECOGNITION

Acknowledgment fuels engagement, but only when it reflects genuine contribution rather than noise. Reward impact over visibility.

SKILL MOBILITY & EXPANSION

Rotate responsibilities, upskill, and challenge minds. Growth is sustained when curiosity meets opportunity.

DECISIVE CONFLICT PROTOCOLS

Conflict becomes constructive when the process is clear. Unresolved tension corrodes focus and decision-making.

SAFE WORKING ENVIRONMENT

Zero tolerance for harassment or intimidation is non-negotiable. Security of mind and body is a prerequisite for cognitive excellence.

AUTONOMY IN EXECUTION

Control over where, when, and how work happens preserves mental bandwidth and supports high-caliber output.

EMOTIONAL LITERACY

Teams that detect and decode emotional signals navigate ambiguity and collaboration more effectively, avoiding silent friction.

DESIGNATED RECHARGE SPACES

Opportunities to reset attention are essential. Downtime is not indulgence; it's the currency of sharp thinking. The right structure plans, does the heavy lifting, and leaves minds free to decide, not scramble.

Embed these principles to create a workplace that doesn't just survive fatigue; it engineers consistent mental performance. Regular refinement ensures the framework evolves alongside the people it governs.

MONITORING AND OPTIMIZATION

Good intentions are not enough. Intentions without measurement are invisible. Performance thrives when structures, flow, and outcomes are continuously examined and fine-tuned.

EARLY STRAIN INDICATORS: Identify bottlenecks, interruptions, and friction points that silently sap cognitive bandwidth.

TASK FLOW ANALYSIS: Visualize work distribution to uncover hidden overloads, inefficiencies, and decision risks.

SYSTEM INTEGRATION: Evaluate contributions based on clarity, judgment, and ownership, not noise or verbal dominance.

COLLABORATION HEALTH: Measure the quality of teamwork, conflict resolution, and idea synthesis to ensure collective intelligence is optimized.

Systems teach before leaders speak.
What they reward consistently earns attention.

RECOGNITION EFFECTIVENESS: Gauge whether acknowledgment truly motivates and reinforces behaviors that drive impact.

SCHEDULE IMPACT ASSESSMENT: Test how alternative rhythm, deep work blocks, asynchronous collaboration, compressed weeks, influence outcomes and alignment.

LEARNING RETURNS: Track application of knowledge from workshops, interventions, or mentoring programs to verify that insights translate into decisions.

RESOURCE UTILIZATION: Monitor how focus-enhancing environments, digital tools, or quiet zones are leveraged to preserve cognitive stamina.

CLIMATE CHECKS: Assess clarity, psychological safety, and alignment to detect systemic gaps that erode performance before they manifest.

BENEFIT IMPACT: Evaluate whether support structures, autonomy options, ergonomic adjustments, and cognitive aids genuinely enhance sustained output.

Outcomes follow frameworks. Structure writes the story.

Optimizing is not about tracking busywork; it is about unlocking hidden potential, maximizing performance, and turning insight into consistent execution.

Measurement becomes a strategic lever, not a box to check.

CHAPTER 7 - QUIZ

Answer honestly, no corporate PR spin. At the end, tally your points to see if your organization unlocks focus, sabotages it, or hovers somewhere in between.

Is Your Workplace
Quietly Draining or Amplifying Talent?
Keep an eye on the signals, not the slogans.

1. Work Environment
a) Quiet zones, private offices, or focus pods exist and are respected. (3 points)
b) Mostly open-plan, but a few escape routes exist. (2 points)
c) Open space everywhere; silence is a myth. (1 point)

2. Meetings & Collaboration
a) One-on-one, asynchronous, and group options are standard. (3 points)
b) Mostly group meetings, occasional written follow-ups. (2 points)
c) Meetings are loud, lively, and everyone must speak up. (1 point)

3. Feedback Culture

a) Private, constructive, and personalized feedback is routine. (3 points)

b) Mix of private and public feedback; consistency is patchy. (2 points)

c) Feedback happens in front of everyone, often reactive. (1 point)

4. Social Engagement

a) Optional events, small gatherings, and thoughtful inclusion. (3 points)

b) Large-team events dominate; optional participation is rare. (2 points)

c) Mandatory fun; introversion optional. (1 point)

5. Autonomy & Scheduling

a) Employees control hours, task order, and location. (3 points)

b) Some flexibility, but rigid deadlines and time rules still dominate. (2 points)

c) Fixed schedules, rigid workflow, no deviation allowed. (1 point)

6. Communication Style

a) Multiple channels available: email, chat, boards, async tools. (3 points)

b) Some written tools exist, but live conversations dominate. (2 points)

c) Everything happens in real-time; speaking fast is valued over being understood. (1 point)

7. Cognitive Recovery

a) Quiet rooms, decompression zones, or reset rituals are part of the culture. (3 points)

b) Occasional encouragement to take breaks; spaces are limited. (2 points)

c) Burnout is normal; there are no structures for mental reset. (1 point)

8. Development & Growth

a) Learning paths adapt to working style; solo or small-group options exist. (3 points)

b) Mostly group training; some individual customization. (2 points)

c) One-size-fits-all development; individuality ignored. (1 point)

SCORES

21–24 points:
PERFORMANCE AMPLIFIER

Your company nurtures quiet brilliance. Cognitive bandwidth is preserved, introverted talent thrives, and sustained contribution is visible.

13–20 points:
MIXED SIGNALS

Your organization does some things well, but leaks energy in key places. Identify friction points and test structural changes to preserve focus.

8–12 points:
SILENT DRAIN

Your workplace unintentionally erodes cognitive performance. Quiet contributors are losing ground. It's time to rethink environment, autonomy, and recovery systems.

HR DECODER:
SPEAK FLUENT WORKPLACE

Not every HR term rolls off the tongue. Here's your cheat sheet to decode the lingo. Quick, sharp, and operational, this is your backstage pass to HR jargon without the head-scratching.

Cut the fluff. Nail the meaning. Master the moves.

Task Masking: When employees hide true workload or effort to appear on track.

Boomerang Employee: Someone who returns to a former organization, bringing fresh perspective and retained knowledge.

Cognitive Bandwidth: The mental "*space*" available to process information, make decisions, and execute work.

Psychological Safety: The trust that speaking up or making mistakes won't carry personal risk.

Structural Optionality: Systems, schedules, and workflows designed so employees can choose how and when they contribute.

Signal vs. Noise: Distinguishing meaningful insight from distracting activity or chatter.

Quiet Multiplier: The cumulative effect of thoughtful, deliberate, and measured contributions across a team or organization.

Alignment Interaction: Check-ins and touchpoints that ensure energy and effort are directed toward agreed priorities.

Recovery Governance: Practices and policies that protect employees' mental and cognitive recharge.

Entry Point Multiplication: Providing multiple channels for ideas and feedback to ensure all contributions surface.

Career Cushioning: Strategies employees use to safeguard future growth or stability, often by diversifying skills or networks.

Virtual Buffering: Intentional digital boundaries that reduce cognitive strain in remote or hybrid environments.

Energy Flex: Adjusting personal effort and focus across tasks and time to maintain sustainable output.

Attention Anchors: Habits, rituals, or tools that ground focus amid distractions and shifting priorities.

Now that you have all the tools, you are ready to lead change and champion introverts by celebrating their unique strengths.

Together, we can dispel misconceptions and empower introverts to unleash their Quiet Brilliance.

"Silence is the new loud,
and authenticity is our battle cry."

Sara Yahia

ABOUT THE AUTHOR

Sara Yahia is a powerhouse in human resources, a trailblazing author, and a champion for inclusive workplaces. With over a decade of global HR leadership, she has transformed organizations by designing environments where talent thrives, not just survives.

A multiple award winner, Sara combines strategic insight with a deep understanding of introverted talent, helping companies unlock focus, depth, and innovation.

Author of *Quietly Sparks*, *Quiet Diversity*, and *Unheard Voices*, she turns research, experience, and wit into actionable guidance for leaders who want results without forcing performance theater.

Sara regularly shares her expertise in *Forbes*, *People Management Magazine*, *TalentCulture*, *HR Executive*, *HR Today*, *ET HR World*, *Khaleej Times*, and *HR.com*, shaping conversations on the future of work.

She is a sought-after consultant and advisor, known for making complex HR and DEI strategies bold, practical, and impossible to ignore.

Lead Smarter and Turn Ideas into Impact!

Scan Here!

REFERENCES

American Psychological Association. (2023). *Stress in America: The State of Our Nation*. https://www.apa.org/news/press/releases/stress/2023

Baicker, K., Cutler, D., & Song, Z. (2010). *Workplace Wellness Programs Can Generate Savings*. Health Affairs, 29(2), 304-311. https://www.healthaffairs.org/doi/full/10.1377/hlthaff.2009.0626

Bloom, N., Liang, J., Roberts, J., & Ying, Z. J. (2015). *Does Working from Homework? Evidence from a Chinese Experiment*. Quarterly Journal of Economics, 130(1), 165-218. https://academic.oup.com/qje/article/130/1/165/2384907

Cain, S. (2012). *Quiet: The Power of Introverts in a World That Can't Stop Talking*. Crown Publishing Group.

Gallup. (2017). *State of the American Workplace Report*. https://www.gallup.com/workplace/238085/state-american-workplace-report-2017.aspx

Gallup. (2021). *State of the Global Workplace: 2021 Report*. https://www.gallup.com/workplace/349484/state-global-workplace.aspx

Gassam Asare, J. (2025, November 5). *Mamdani's win may lead to a spike in Islamophobia: Here's how companies can tackle it head-on. Forbes*.

https://www.forbes.com/sites/janicegassam/2025/11/05/mamdanis-win-may-lead-to-a-spike-in-islamophobia-hereshow-companies-can-tackle-it-head-on/

Helgoe, L. (2008). *Introvert Power: Why Your Inner Life Is Your Hidden Strength*. Sourcebooks.

Kahnweiler, J. B. (2013). *Quiet Influence: The Introvert's Guide to Making a Difference*. Berrett-Koehler Publishers.

Kim, J., & de Dear, R. (2013). *Workspace Satisfaction: The Privacy-Communication Trade-Off in Open-Plan Offices*. Journal of Environmental Psychology, 36, 18-26.

Laney, M. O. (2002). *The Introvert Advantage: How Quiet People Can Thrive in an Extrovert World*. Workman Publishing Company.

Laurie, H., & Swanson, L. (2021). *The Introvert Advantage in Modern Work Environments*. Journal of Organizational Behavior, 42(2), 221-239.

Mayne, M. (2025, December 18). *From 'quiet cracking' to 'culture rot': The workplace trends that defined 2025*. People Management. https://www.peoplemanagement.co.uk/article/1943529/quiet-cracking-culture-rot-workplace-trends-defined-2025

Roberts, L. M., Mayo, A. J., & Thomas, D. A. (2018). *Race, Work, and Leadership: New Perspectives on the Black Experience*. Harvard Business Review Press.

Steelcase. *The Privacy Crisis: Taking a Toll on Employee Engagement.* https://www.steelcase.com/eu-en/research/articles/topics/privacy/privacy-crisis/

Smith, J., Zhang, Y., & Adams, R. (2019). *Introverts in the Workplace: A Study on Performance and Job Satisfaction.* University of California Press.

Yahia, S. (2023). *Quietly Sparks: Inner Power in a Loud Realm.* Amazon Publishing.

QUIET DIVERSITY

*A Guide to Cultivating
Introvert-Friendly Workplaces*

SARA YAHIA